Poems after the Watershed

P. F. Mitchell

Author's note:

Not suitable reading for children: teenagers in a rush: adults easily upset or embarrassed by matters of the world and body: old age pensioners on a tight financial budget: literary critics.

www.fast-print.net/store.php

POEMS AFTER THE WATERSHED

All characters are fictional. Any similarity to any actual person is purely coincidental

ISBN 978-184426-867-2

First published 2010 by
FASTPRINT PUBLISHING
Peterborough, England.

An environmentally friendly book printed and bound in England by
www.printondemand-worldwide.com

This book is made entirely of chain-of-custody materials

"A book of poems that actually rhyme is very novel"
Author

" I've moved into the *spare bedroom"*
Author's wife

" I want a DNA test"
Author's eldest daughter

" Why do parents always let you down"
Author's youngest daughter

" I only read a small extraction, but it will fill a cavity in my bookshelf"
Author's dentist

" You won't get away with this stuff"
Author's ex-mate

" A well matured plot with plenty of room for further growth"
Author's allotment friend

" I knew marrying into this family was a mistake"
Author's son-in-law

" Never heard of this bloke"
Poets Guild

CONTENTS

The Pain of Love

My eyes are bulging with constant stare
As she glides towards me with flick of hair
My mouth is dry I can hardly speak
As she smiles with warmth and rosy cheek

My throat is rough I feel a wreck
As she just strokes her swan like neck
My heart beats faster my chest is tight
As she shows her cleavage what a sight

My stomach's churning in an awful mess
As she flashes a tattoo beneath her dress
My loin is aching is that something stirring
As she sits on my lap like a pussy cat purring

My hands tremble exploring her charms
As she holds me tight within her arms
My legs go weak my feet loose their feeling
As she takes me now I could reach the ceiling

So I need an answer to life's big question
Is this really love……or acid indigestion

My Nanny

I once had a nanny
As my parents couldn't cope
She was at least six foot two
And smelt of rancid soap

I never knew if she was born
Invented, or lost at sea
I really had no idea
She frightened the hell out of me

With a head full of warts
Moles, pocks and pits
Her gummy toothless grin
Used to give me the shits

With large broad shoulders
And a forty eight inch neck
Plus two enormous boobs
That almost scraped the deck

With a belly so fat
And a bum ten foot wide
When she let off wind
It actually turned the tide

A hundred fags a day
Made her periods disappear
She just had a fall of soot
About three times a year

With legs like tree trunks
And feet like flippers
She couldn't wear shoes
Just size fourteen slippers

She dribbled in my face
As she tickled my tummy
Help me God I'd shout
I just want my mummy

A Builder's Bum

My brother is a builder
And he has a builder's bum
It's deep dark and hairy
And right opposite his tum

He takes it to work each day
His only pride and joy
He's always wanted a builder's bum
Since he was a little boy

He takes it with him everywhere
Up ladders, scaffolding and planks
It's something to sit on
While fitting tubing, pipes and tanks

It has a sunny outlook
As it watches all the girls go by
And often smiles and winks at them
With it's only eye

Some girls laugh and giggle
And like to take the piss
Just don't stand too close
When it blows a kiss

Hammer, nails and screwdriver
Are really useful tools
But you can't beat a builder's bum
When you're making stools

Now when its time is over
And God calls that deadly strike
I'm going to burying it in my garden
So I can park my bike

Beerbellyman

Unshaven, bald and eight months pregnant
Trousers hitched around a sixty inch waist
Shirt buttons straining under the pressure
Indeed a man, but not to every woman's taste

Waddling along, hips sway from side to side
Blocks pavements, in doorways always stuck
From front or back it's really much the same
He looks just like a giant constipated duck

You often see him mingling with the herd
Supping at his favourite watering hole
Downing pints of lager till closing time
Then in the morning off to collect the dole

Doesn't like to exercise, or work up a sweat
Likes a game of pool, or to throw a set of darts
Won't cut the grass, or help around the house
Eats like a horse, and has very similar farts

He slobbers kisses on the wife, God help her
Wanting sex, his belly sticking like a leech
She has no need to worry, or move away
His four inch thing is never going to reach

My Favourite Swear Word

Swearing isn't very smart
And It's awfully rude
Although I am an old fart
I'm certainly not a prude

Swearing is a fact of life
And has a useful purpose
The relief of stress and strife
When other words are surplus

Most people have a favourite word
Like those that start with F or C
Popular with the common herd
But not my cup of tea

So when people get on my tit
I don't say arse or bum
Not even boobs or shit
I just shout out….. scrotum

The Cruise

When I have a holiday
I do like a long sea cruise
Lots of sun, food and sites
Plus some fags and booze

I only go with the old folks
So book my trip with Saga
They don't mind if I remove my teeth
To soak in a pint of lager

I'm happy on a big cruise liner
Or just a little boat
As long as it has a bar
And hopefully stays afloat

Lots to do no time to waste
I even play the bingo
All the fours those droopy drawers
I just love the sexy lingo

I like to take the fresh sea air
As I hobble along the decks
Watching all the world sail by
As I chat to the other wrecks

In sandals and shorts I wander
Looking for the next sight of docks
But if it gets any dam hotter
I may take off my socks

It Comes to us all - or not

I still think of sex as I get older
But have lost my youthful ardour
The wife has noticed and often says
Won't the dam thing go any harder

I've even taken it in both hands
For a little physical persuasion
It began to stir and smile
But wouldn't rise to the occasion

I bought a mag from the top shelf
And spread open at the centre fold
Gemma with a thirty six inch bust
But even her beauty left me cold

I went to the doctors in despair
He diagnosed erectile dysfunction
He said it was common at my age
Not to get it up the junction

So as a very last resort
I took that stuff they call Viagra
Trust me to get an adverse reaction
And spend the night peeing like Niagara

A Book at Bedtime

Whilst browsing in my local book shop
Looking for a manual to fix the car
I came across a book on Indian Art
It was called the Karma Sutra

Opening the book I very soon saw
It wasn't about paintings or musicians
Not even modern or ancient history
But having sex in different positions

I was surprised as I thumbed the pages
Came across a picture that made me frown
It didn't seem to make much sense at first
Until I turned the book upside down

Now sex is fun but very tiring
Especially at my time of life
But hope springs eternal in us all
So I took it home to show the wife

I placed it on the coffee table
Well within her reach and sight
So I took a chance and softly whispered
Why don't we have an early night

Went to the bathroom to prepare myself
Brushed my tooth and combed my hair
Removed my socks, long johns and vest
Laid down beside her totally bare

Then she spoke those words I'd heard before
That dim the ardour with desire diminished
Don't take too long or wake me up
And pull down my nightie when you've finished

Hello I'm on the Bus

I haven't got a car nor a credit card
No overdraft and certainly not one of these
I don't take drugs or drink too hard
I lead a simple life and do just as I please

People say you don't have to smoke a joint
But it's never too late to learn to drive
I say thanks but what's the point
I passed my test in nineteen sixty five

Oh no we have no kids some couples utter
I don't stir or even blink an eye
One day I might get brave and mutter
Why don't you both give sex a try

Buying stuff on plastic is really just a joke
It's something stupid I couldn't master
The banks get rich but you get stony broke
So the whole dam thing ends up in disaster

Hello I'm on the bus booms that awful drone
Who cares about your life or that nasty spot
So whoever invented the ruddy mobile phone
Should be sent to jail, or better still be shot

Santa's Coming

Across the sky the sound of hooves
Then a sleigh appears in a sudden flash
It's Santa and his herd of reindeer
Over the chimney tops in a dash

No time to waste can't stop now
Far too much to see and do
He's bringing lots of tacky gifts
To every Chav plus me and you

Rudolph's nose is shining bright and red
So all can see them as they pass
It's his own fault really he has been told
Not to get so close to Santa's arse

Playboy Annuals and page three calendars
Plus the latest blow up doll for the boys
While the girls like smelly perfume
Not to mention those vibrating sex toys

Presents aren't what they used to be
Now it's all smut something shocking
Thank God Santa only comes once a year
But at least he fills your stocking

Thoughts

What could I think of at a time like this
My favourite tune, was it a hit or miss

I scanned my memory for a long lost thought
Something treasured, stolen, or bought

How about the greatest goal, try or wicket
I could blow my nose, scratch or pick it

Rubbish on the telly with nothing to see
Why do I bother to pay the fee

Bankers are greedy, politicians on the make
What's happening to the world for goodness sake

The planet's in a mess thanks to planes and cars
Wonder what the house prices are like on Mars

Getting desperate thinking of motorway cones
Then at last it came with the sound of moans

So I smiled and grinned with great elation
I'd managed to cure my premature ejaculation

Why do we do it

I awake on Monday morning
My brain in a total haze
I went to bed on Friday
I seem to have lost two days

My head is pounding thunder
Both eyes shoot lightning bright
I try to focus on the room
That wallpapers an awful sight

I try to breathe to stay alive
With a nose that's big and sore
My shirt is stained with blood
There's more on the bedroom door

My mouth is full of sandpaper
Breath like a budgie's fart
I must look in the mirror
But I really don't have the heart

Why do we do it I always ask
It only causes pain and strife
But if you think I sound a mess
You should see the bingeing wife

Nature

Nature is a wondrous thing
Created for all mankind
The small, the tall, the thin
The seeing and the blind

No matter what your colour
Birth place, class or creed
You're only on this earth
To live, survive and breed

No one cares how you live
Cave, house or apartment block
If you stand alone, chase the herd
Or be part of the shepherd's flock

Across the planet, east to west
North to south and pole to pole
The survival of mankind
Is your only overriding goal

Money's great to borrow
Steal, spend, give away or to save
But you can't take it with you
To your cold and lonely grave

provide food and shelter for yourself
And hopefully find a mate
And don't forget it's also natures way
To eat, sleep and procreate

Some seek fame and fortune
Or crave an overnight sensation
Much better to have contributed
To mankind's next generation

Forget fighting, war and crime
Just fulfil your human instinct
Or like the dinosaur and dodo
We will all become extinct

Worship where and who you like
There must be a thousand Gods
But there is no greater gift in life
Than when a women pods

Broken Britain's got the Yob Factor

You see them most day and night
Some people call them yobs
Boy spelt backward sounds about right
No sense, no hope, no jobs

You rarely see them on their own
They're not that brave at one to one
But in a group they grunt and groan
Lost is the desire to just have fun

Stripped of fashion, they all look the same
Sloppy jeans, baseball caps and hoods
Can't show their faces for the shame
Hide in the shadows, alleys and woods

Smoke a lot, but can't hold their drink
Both parents teach them how to curse
Hooked on drugs, unable to think
Their days just go from bad to worse

But they can't be yobs for ever and ever
Most will have to make a career decision
What to do, when you're mouthy not clever
Banker, estate agent, or even a politician

The Garden of Life

When life gets you down
You don't want to talk
No light in the tunnel
Just pick up a fork
If the noise gets too loud
Block out the sound
Escape from the rat race
Dig in the ground
Release pent up emotion
By pulling up a weed
Achieve inner fulfilment
By planting a seed
As it all gets too much
This struggle and toil
When the tears start to fall
Let them water the soil
If you feel useless
Your mind's full of doubt
Down at your feet
New life starts to sprout
The body may feel weak
Lost its will power
But it's all down to you
Your seed's now a flower
Life makes you punch drunk
You just want to howl
Please take my advice
Don't throw in the trowel

It's far too Late

Life's not a rehearsal you've heard it said
It's far too late when you're gone and dead

Take care of your body, you won't get another
It's far too late when you look like your mother

Remember to be pleasant, funny and kind
It's far too late when age wrecks your mind

Make a new friend, each and every day
It's far too late when life's draining away

Find peace with your mate, or love that's stalled
It's far too late when your name's finally called

Cherish the day your children were born
It's far too late when the curtains are drawn

Live life to the full, whether it be short or long
It's far too late when they sing the last song

Don't leave this world your soul in turmoil
It's far too late when you're dust in the soil

Lost in the City

Stopped by the kerb just past midnight
Must check my map so put on the light

Upon the window came a loud knocking
Appeared a face that was totally shocking

Looking fors a good time is yer sailor
No East Street and I'm a gentleman's tailor

Whot suits yer best I heard her mutter
As she slid in beside me from the gutter

I seem to be lost, I'm new to this city
Nay mind me duck wanna feel me titty

Does yer wants it straight, or summit kinky
Or yous can put yer hand upon me pinkie

Does yer want a spanking, ors just a screw
Please no, directions to East Street will do

Yous can ties me up or down, or hav a sixty nine
For pity's sake young lady, East Street is fine

Pay for whot yer want, I's told yer whot I did
Turn left for East Street, so that be twenty quid

I'm not Obese, Just Bloody Fat

My face is red and very chubby
And my chins are far too many
I just wish I could see my feet
When I need to spend a penny

I certainly don't have bat wings
More like top sails that hoist
My underarms are deepest caves,
Smelly, hairy, dark and moist

My boobs are like mountains
My poor old bra can't cope
And when it starts to snow
You can ski down each slope

There are lots of uses for my chest
Plus that overhanging belly
Like balancing a plate of chips
While watching crap on the telly

My private part is also huge
And not just for pissing
But the last man who entered there
Has been reported missing

My bottom is rather large,
And sticks out about three feet
When I have a call of nature
Only the hole fits on the seat

Clothes are quite a problem
When you're the size of a bus
My Tops are from Mostyn Curtains
I get my frocks from Tents-R-Us

My knickers are far too big,
You really ought to see em
There's a pair on display
In the London Science Museum

I've tried support stockings
But they wouldn't hold
So now I use bits of string
And a piece of iron scaffold

Shoes would be really nice
Or even a pair of sandals
Till then I'll use some buckets
And hold onto the handles

I don't know what to do
To over-eating I may be prone
So shall I start the diet this year
Or wait till I top thirty stone

The Good Ship Phallic

Was on the good ship *Phallic*
As the call rang out for battle
They all stood naked on the deck
Both hands upon their tackle

The Captain bellowed at the crew
We'll have a kit inspection
I'll flog the dog whose weapon's bent
And not wearing any protection

Boson Grimes was an ugly bugger
With a face full of yellow puss
But down below he stood out proud
Somewhere to hang his cutlass

The mid-shipman was short and stout
But could fill any utensil
He'd often use it as a paper weight
And sometimes as a pencil

The galley cook without his apron
Wasn't used to standing bare
Didn't like the thought of roasted chestnuts
Nor the smell of singeing hair

The gunner had a twelve inch cannon
Plus two enormous iron balls
Watch out when he relieves himself
As it's just like Niagara falls

Cockney Dick lived up to his name
As it swung down between his legs
When it got wet he just wrung it out
Then hung it up with pegs

Jock had to clean and paint the woodwork
Then polish all the brass
The scrubber fell off his two foot pole
So he had to use his arse

Paddy was from Dublin
With the cutest leprechaun you've ever seen
On St Patrick's day it would do a gig
All painted in emerald green

John Thomas was from Wales
With a voice that made men weep
He had another gift at the other end
That required a flock of sheep

Up the mast was Tiny Tim the cabin boy
Just trying to do his best
Being Small and limp wasn't his fault
He's yet to reach the nest

The ship's doctor had seen them all before
And taken a few in hand
His case comes up before the courts
Next time they reach dry land

What's in a Name

The Aussies like to call us Poms
Yanks just shout out Limey
English, Paddies, Taffs and Jocks
What a bunch cor blimey

Scousers, Geordies and the Brummies
All belong to a different gang
Try understanding a Cockney
When he spouts that funny slang

Now we're all in Europe we have to mix
With Frogs, Iti, Spanyard and Polocks
But to say we mean them harm
Is just a load of bolocks

It's cold up north and white as snow
Where Swedes and Danes are fair
Ruskies also wrap up warm
Especially if there's a Nip in the air

We've had a bargie with the Argies
Some Brazilians are nuts
Would we live with a Chile willy
Do Peruvians hate our guts

What's in a name just ask yourself
What were you called at school
Rise above the common herd
Don't be a name caller like a fool

Some names don't sound too nice
Like Paki, Kraut and Chink
But mostly spoken without malice
We just forgot to think

In a land that's free of thought
We have our say with loud of voice
Not to like certain things and people
Is our individual right of choice

To preach abuse, think we are superior
And then act as if we are
Is when we're called a racist
Then you know we've gone too far

Sticks and stones may our break our bones
But names will never hurt a Brit
As long as we're not called late for dinner
We don't really give a shit

Going South

As your wife gets old and grey
Her body parts start dropping
Bags beneath her eyes flap in the wind
They come in handy for the shopping

She tries to look her best
When going to a dance or function
Try slapping on the war paint
With a face like Clapham Junction

Out come the diamond ear rings
Not to wear them would be a sin
There is a diamond necklace
Somewhere beneath her treble chin

Her breasts used to be firm and plump
Made for children and men to squeeze
Now long and thin like razor strops
Dangling an inch below her knees

There is this sinking feeling when she sits
Upon the bar stool in the pub
The beers not all that's overflowing
She's joined the saggy bottom club

My private part is still intact
She cries with pure amazement
I'm not sure that's really true
Is that a crack upon the pavement

Make Plans

Make plans for this world
You've not long to stay
The long term or short term
Not just from day to day

This world is a mystery
Makes you laugh or cry
When you just day dream
Life passes you by

There is only the future
The past is now waning
You can't help what's gone
Can you change what's coming

Nothing will get better
If you take no action
Get your life in order
To achieve inner satisfaction

Save time for relaxation
Plan time for working
Watch time if you must
But make time for laughing

Don't worry about fate
Live or die is just an even bet
Make sure your plans succeed
Don't look back with regret

They say…I say

They say absence makes the heart
Grow fonder
I say don't go home at all
Just wander

They say I believe in love
At first sight
I say keep the bag on her head
Except at night

They say beauty is in the eye
Of the beholder
I say the ugly ones are more
Eager and bolder

They say love is a many
Splendour thing
I say don't bother just buy
Her bling

They say you can't judge a book
By the cover
I say give up reading and
Take a lover

They say you have to watch
The quiet ones
I say I like them noisy when I
Squeeze their buns

They say I like them tall, dark
And handsome
I say be thankful for what you get
Or be lonesome

They say I like a sense of humour
Size doesn't matter
I say you won't laugh at mine, when it
Makes you fatter

They say a bird in the hand is worth
Two in the bush
I say a bird with a bush is worth
A hand

Woolly the Woofter

I woke up this morning
To the start of another day
Still feeling tired and sleepy
Or was it dopey, happy or doc
Hi ho it's off to work I go
I'm just a little gay
Shall I wear my tight new pants
Or the yellow floral frock

Put on my two bob watch
But what lipstick do I choose
Got to look my best
When I kneel before the Queen
This shirt really needs a lift
To go with the high heeled shoes
When I walk the High Street
I do like to cause a scene

I like to take the fresh sea air
As I walk along the pier
But the wind gets up these parts
It's really heaven sent
The waves go up and down
And make me feel a little queer
So I'll hold onto the railings
No matter if their bent

Feeling peckish, time for lunch
For a bit of what I fancy
A cucumber sandwich, lemon tart
Followed by a creamy fairy cake
Sipping tea with Sandy
Simon, Julian and Nancy
Ben Down and Phil McCavity
Also known as Hairy Jake

Titus Arsen is from Holland
And is my camping mate
We put up the tent, grease the pole
Then set off for a hike
He ran down to the shore
Shouting the tide it won't wait
Then just stood there smiling
With his finger in the local dyke

I've had a very busy day
All this talking and mincing
Now it's getting rather late
The night is drawing near
Along the straight and narrow
I'll take some convincing
Home again, forgot my key
So I'll enter by the rear

Speling

Now speling isnt my strongest piont
I get things rong and people frown
I dont mind saying words out lowd
But cant get them rite wen writen down

Hert my finger the other mourning
It bleded a lot and could turn sceptic
Sore the Doctor Who dressed the cut
Then gave me a doss of sum antibionic

My sister dus biologee at skool
Diseks frogs to watch them spasem
Looks thru microwskops to sea indetail
Says she always liked a little orgasm

My favorit book is Sherlok Homes
Solvin murders by dager or gun
He always gets the gilty criminal
It's just alimentary deer Whatsun

My mate whent out to a niteclub
Drunk to much and becam inoculated
Caused a sceen and hit a bounser
Sow had to be forcefuly ejaculated

My brother thinks he's not that clever
To get more lerning its never to late
He wants to take a nite skool cors
So hes off to the colege to masturbate

I'm very prowd of my many plants
I grow them myself, I find it cheeper
Sum are small but sum are hugh
You shood see the siz of my vagina creeper

The wife whent to the store with my note
Turned out to be quit a funny tail
Dont know why the sailsman larfed
As I only wanted a six foot dildo rail

My Calendar

January starts the brand new year
All hopes of joy, perhaps a little fear
On shortest day my voice does sing
I wonder what this year will bring

February is a month that's cold
It's short, so let my heart be bold
Make plans for when spring is here
Keep contact with those I hold dear

March winds blow and chill the bone
Visit the old folks or pick up the phone
Will the sun ever shine I often say
I see the daffodils and their golden ray

April showers dappen the ground
Animals stirring is the new sound
Out and about to take in the fresh air
A walk in the forest with a love I share

May blossoms paint all the trees bright
A month to savour, a wondrous sight
Book up a holiday, I do need a break
Look forward to life for goodness sake

June is already half way there
Pray for that sunshine if I dare
Get out that swimsuit it may still fit
Off to the seaside with my sand castle kit

July is for children, enjoy every day
Turn off the telly and go out to play
Half past nine but I can still see
Relax in the twilight under the tree

August is a nothing month for me
Part summer, part autumn it seems to be
I have this bad feeling, what is the reason
Oh no it can't be the football season

September is a month I love to hate
My summer jobs I've left too late
Next year will do, so stop my bleating
A bit too early to switch on the heating

October heralds the autumn hue
The cobwebs sparkle with the dew
Air so pure it can't be tinned
A golden snow drifts in the wind

November is a month I really dread
Those Christmas songs mess up my head
I wish I'd booked a winter cruise
To get away from the Santa blues

December comes far too fast I feel
Another year gone, it can't be real
Look back in joy or just reflect a bit
Mourn my friends, who didn't make it

Have Gun will Travel

Off into town with my mate Percy
Hear the girls scream and beg for mercy
I'm not that bright, most say I'm thick
Walking the streets holding hands with Dick

Here he comes, with joy the desperate sob
That upper class hunk they call the nob
No time to think, you have to be quick
It's a first come basis for this prick

Book your service in my motor pool
For every position I have the tool
If you fancy a single or double decker
I'll punch your ticket with my pecker

Makes you speechless, a real word stopper
When get your tongue around this chopper
You have to be strong to last the course
Bare back riding with hung like a horse

So all of you, of the lonely female gender
See the rates for my upstanding member
Just a man for hire, I'm a real cinch
Not rented by the hour, but by the inch

Where we live

You live in a white thatched cottage
With red roses over a garden gate
I live in a grey concrete box
Upon a murky British sink estate

You breath country air that's fresh
With just a hint of a wooden fire
All I smell is danger and despair
With just the hint of a burning tyre

Farmyard animals roam your fields
Cows, horses, sheep, pigs and hogs
Pit bull walkers foul my pavement
Closely followed by their dogs

Your winding lanes are full of colour
With buttercup and foxglove clashing
I have coloured lights along my road
But they are always blue and flashing

Little old shops around a village green
Windows full of ribbons and silk
Our row of shops are boarded up
Can't even buy a pint of milk

Just be thankful to be fit and well
And live the life that's dealt to you
Make the most of what gifts you have
It's not where you live but what you do

Gee-Zero-Delta…………Chapter One

Soil scorched by the heat
All now turned to dust
Buildings start to topple
Through the cracks in the crust
Food and water running low
And nowhere to shelter
On a far away doomed planet
Called Gee-Zero-Delta

Planet won't last much longer
In its present bad state
A new hope and beginning
The Lords need to create
A search of the galaxy
Then found a dead star
Six million light years away
Not really that far

Void of all signs of life
And shrouded in darkness
The Lords started to build
In their very own likeness
To give day and night
A new sun is at hand
Siphon off some water
To give up dry land

Chapter Two

The new planet was ready
After four generations
Time to move creatures
To their new stations
Scatter the planet with fruit
That's good and self-seeding
Watch the grass grow
And the animals breeding

Beings were now needed
To build and to toil
Watch over the animals
And tend to the soil
But the Sons of Gee-Zero-Delta
They no longer mate
Just clone when needed
At a sensible rate

So a Lord was despatched
To manage the project
Creating some new beings
That was his object
He first cloned a male
From right off the shelf
From a bone in the body
He stem-celled herself

Chapter Three

After six long generations
The new planet set fair
With fish in the sea
And birds in the air
Animals roamed freely
Forests covered the ground
To a brand new beginning
The Lords were now bound

As the new beings multiplied
And had daughters fair
The Sons of Gee-Zero-Delta
They wanted their share
Mixing with the beings
Brought forth new life
But created mankind
With trouble and strife

The mass evacuation was ready
But suddenly put on hold
Bad things were happening
A Lord's messenger told
The Lords and Sons listened
To a violent and sad situation
The new planet wasn't fit
For their lasting habitation

Chapter Four

The Lords frowned and grieved
At the planet they had created
Inter-breeding was now rife
And brought forth evil unabated
Giant beasts strode the land
Which were not in the plan
So the order went out to destroy
All the new creatures and man

The Lords selected one family
For hope and mankind's sake
To start afresh on the planet
And right the previous mistake
Gather up all creatures
That are worthy and clean
Enter a boat to escape
The coming devastating scene

Siphoned off sea was returned
Crashing down in huge waves
All living things perished
In their watery graves
Only one righteous family
Lived to tell the tale
When the Lords sent forth death
Through rain, snow and hail

Chapter Five

A second new beginning
Arose from the haze
Where the Lords could spend
Their very last days
With a Lord and his Sons
Each space ship was filled
As Gee-Zero-Delta exploded
Its existence was stilled

The new planet needed populating
In each and every part
So the ships took up beings
To make a fresh start
Mankind was then spread
Throughout the vast land
To build new life and language
A Lord was at hand

With the passing of the old
And beginning of the new
Mankind was plentiful
But the Lords were now few
A written record was kept
Of the whole operation
So the work of the Lord's
Could be read by a new generation
The End

ND - #0276 - 080726 - C0 - 197/132/4 - PB - 9781844268672 - Gloss Lamination